CHEESE

Edible

Series Editor: Andrew F. Smith

EDIBLE is a revolutionary new series of books dedicated to food and drink that explores the rich history of cuisine. Each book reveals the global history and culture of one type of food or beverage.

Already published

Chocolate Sarah Moss and Alexander Badenoch

Curry Colleen Taylor Sen

Hamburger Andrew F. Smith

Hot Dog Bruce Kraig

Pancake Ken Albala

Pie Janet Clarkson

Pizza Carol Helstosky

Spices Fred Czarra

Forthcoming

Beer Bob Skilnik

Bread William Rubel

Cake Nicola Humble

Caviar Nichola Fletcher

Champagne Becky Sue Epstein

Cocktails Joseph M. Carlin

Coffee Jonathan Morris

Corn Linda Murray Berzok

Dates Nawal Nasrallah

Fish and Chips Panikos Panayi

Gin Lesley Jacobs Solmonson

Ice Cream Laura Weiss

Lobster Elisabeth Townsend

Milk Hannah Velten

Pasta Kantha Shelke

Potato Andrew F. Smith

Soup Janet Clarkson

Tea Helen Saberi

Tomato Deborah A. Duchon

Vodka Patricia Herlihy

Whiskey Kevin R. Rosar

Wine Marc Millon

Cheese

A Global History

Andrew Dalby

REAKTION BOOKS

Published by Reaktion Books Ltd
33 Great Sutton Street
London EC1V 0DX, UK
www.reaktionbooks.co.uk

First published 2009

Printed and bound in China by C&C Offset Printing Co., Ltd

British Library Cataloguing in Publication Data

Dalby, Andrew, 1947–
Cheese : a global history. – (Edible)
1. Cheese – History. 2. Cheesemaking – History.
3. Cookery (Cheese)
I. Title II. Series
641.3′73′09-DC22

ISBN: 978 1 86189 523 3

Contents

I

The Cheeseboard

Like a rock that will weather many storms, Parmesan presides over the cheeseboard. It was already famous around 1370 – and it was already what it is today, a hard, aged cow's-milk cheese – when Giovanni Boccaccio in his *Decameron*, for the sake of a good story, invented 'a mountain made of grated *parmigiano* cheese, with people living on it who never did anything but make macaroni and ravioli and cook them in capon broth'. How much earlier its history may go is unknown. A hundred years after Boccaccio, in 1475, Platina's gastronomic handbook *De honesta voluptate et valetudine* counted *parmensis* (its Latin name) as one of the two princely cheeses of Italy. His contemporaries were less certain what to call their favourite hard cheese. The Parmesan style was widespread in the Po valley; some liked the version made at Piacenza, others preferred Lodi, others again gave the credit to Milan. Finally Parma prevailed. By 1519 Parmesan cheese was a cultural cliché in England, mentioned nonchalantly in a school Latin textbook: 'Ye shall eate parmeson chese!' No wonder, because just a few years earlier Pope Julius II had made a present of a hundred Parmesan cheeses to Henry VIII.[1] That was indeed a royal gift. In 1666, when Samuel Pepys and his neighbour saw the Fire of London approaching, they wisely

7

Above, left to right: Manchego, Cheddar, Parmigiano Reggiano, Reblochon, Mozzarella di bufala, Stilton, Mont d'Or; below, left to right: Gruyère, Laguiole, Brie de Meaux, Roquefort, Gorgonzola. Photographed at La Fromagerie, North London.